AVAILABLE NOW
from Lerner Publishing Services!

The *On the Hardwood* series:

Chicago Bulls
Dallas Mavericks
Los Angeles Clippers
Los Angeles Lakers
Miami HEAT
Minnesota Timberwolves
Oklahoma City Thunder
San Antonio Spurs

COMING SOON!

Additional titles in
the *On the Hardwood* series:

Boston Celtics
Brooklyn Nets
Houston Rockets
Indiana Pacers
New York Knicks
Philadelphia 76ers
Portland Trail Blazers
Utah Jazz

To Order • www.lernerbooks.com • 800-328-4929 • fax 800-332-1132

ON THE HARDWOOD

SAN ANTONIO SPURS

PETE BIRLE

On the Hardwood: San Antonio Spurs

MVP Books
2255 Calle Clara
La Jolla, CA 92037

MVP Books is an imprint of Book Buddy Digital Media, Inc., 42982 Osgood Road, Fremont, CA 94539

MVP Books publications may be purchased for
educational, business, or sales promotional use.

Cover and layout design by Jana Ramsay
Copyedited by Susan Sylvia
Photos by Getty Images

ISBN: 978-1-61570-509-2 (Library Binding)
ISBN: 978-1-61570-508-5 (Soft Cover)

TABLE OF CONTENTS

Chapter 1

BIGGER IS BETTER

It was Game 5 of the 1998-99 NBA Finals at Madison Square Garden, and the New York Knicks had a 77-76 lead on the San Antonio Spurs. There was just over a minute to go, and the Knicks had the ball. It looked like New York was going to live to play another day. A Spurs victory didn't seem likely.

The Knicks got the ball to guard Latrell Sprewell, who had scored 25 points in the second half alone. He was guarded by the Spurs' 6'11" Tim Duncan. His options were limited. So he fired a pass out to forward Larry Johnson, who was waiting beyond the three-point line.

If he scored, the Knicks

Texas-Sized
When the Spurs won their first NBA championship in 1999, it took a Texas-sized Game 5 from big man Tim Duncan.

would have gone up by four and The Garden would have erupted. As the 8th and final seed in the Eastern Conference, the Knicks were

Tim Duncan scored 25 points in the second half of Game 5 to lead the Spurs to victory over the Knicks.

a long shot to win the title. But they believed they could do it, and so did their loud fans.

But Johnson's shot with 1:10 left on the clock bounced high off the back rim. Spurs' guard Mario Elie grabbed the rebound and quickly passed the ball to point guard Avery Johnson. San Antonio's 5'11" Johnson was known as "The Little General," for his small size and take-control attitude.

Johnson brought the ball up court and worked his way over to the left wing. The New York crowd chanted "Defense Defense!" as The Garden organist played the familiar chords.

Johnson lobbed a pass down to big man Tim Duncan, who immediately drew the double team. With his fellow seven-foot center David Robinson, the duo became known as the "Twin Towers" for their

Avery Johnson was known as "The Little General" for his size and his take-charge attitude.

overwhelming height. As Robinson attracted the defense's attention, Duncan found forward Sean Elliott at the top of the key. Elliott waited for the defense to shift, which it did. He pump-faked with both the ball and his head, and then headed into the lane. Instead of driving all the way to the basket, though, he found a wide-open Johnson in the corner. The undrafted lefty, who had bounced around the league for the prior 10 years, calmly nailed the 18-foot baseline J.

The Garden went silent, and the Knicks called timeout. After neither team scored on their next possessions, New York found themselves with the ball out of bounds at midcourt with 2.1 seconds to go.

MADISON SQUARE GARDEN

Forward Sean Elliott attempts a layup against the Knicks.

"The Little General"

Avery Johnson, 5'11", was undrafted and had bounced around the league for a decade. But he hit the biggest shot in Spurs history with his game-winner against the Knicks in the 1999 NBA Finals.

Defense Wins Championships

The Spurs held the Knicks to 10 points in the second quarter of Game 1, a record low for the NBA Finals. They also kept the Knicks from scoring more than 20 points in any quarter throughout the entire series.

Guard Charlie Ward, the former Florida State University quarterback, was charged with making the inbound pass. He launched a beauty, hitting Sprewell in stride in the lane. But Sprewell caught it a bit too far under the backboard. He had to dribble out from under the basket. With big men Duncan and Robinson blocking his way, Sprewell was forced to adjust his fall-away jumper at the buzzer. It didn't reach the hoop. As a result, the Spurs had defeated the Knicks four games to one and captured their first NBA championship since joining the league 26 years ago.

Even though the Knicks lacked the

David Robinson rejects a shot attempt by Latrell Sprewell of the Knicks. The Spurs' held the Knicks scoreless for the final three minutes of the series.

services of their injured Hall of Fame center, Patrick Ewing, the series was a lot closer than it looked. But Sprewell and the Knicks were no match for the Spurs' inside game, featuring their Twin Towers of Duncan and Robinson.

In fact, the Spurs were simply too strong and too tall for the Knicks. Never was that more apparent than on the defensive end of the court. The Spurs held the Knicks scoreless for the final three minutes of the series.

"It is fitting because our defense has carried us through the whole year," said Robinson. "This is what we talked about every huddle for the last 10 minutes. Our defense is going

to win the game for us. And it really did."

In Game 1, the Spurs held the Knicks to 10 points in the second quarter, a record low for the NBA Finals. Duncan and Robinson blocked nine shots between them

The Spurs' Twin Towers—David Robinson and Tim Duncan—gave San Antonio an inside game that was tops in the league.

and failed to score more than 20 in any quarter.

After a loss in Game 3, the Spurs came back in Game 4. Together, Duncan and Robinson blocked seven shots, and they had 34 rebounds between them. The entire Knicks team had only 33 rebounds in Game 4.

The drafting of Duncan two years earlier proved to be just what the Spurs, and Robinson, needed. The pairing of Duncan, the All-American from Wake Forest, with "The Admiral" was perfect. Robinson earned "The Admiral" nickname by virtue of his service for The U.S. Naval Academy. Robinson had been trying, without

in Game 2. New York made only 32.9 percent of its shots from the field

Perfect Together

Robinson had been trying to bring the Spurs a title for 10 years. The missing piece was All-American Tim Duncan, who arrived from Wake Forest to help "The Admiral" raise the banner in San Antonio.

success, to bring the Spurs their first championship for the past 10 years.

Two years earlier, Robinson was hurt, the victim of a back injury. Robinson missed all but six games of the 1996-97 season. Coach Bob Hill was replaced 18 games into the year by General Manager Gregg Popovich. The team finished the year 20-62, the worst record in franchise history.

But, the poor showing on the court translated into a terrific off-season. The Spurs won the NBA's Draft Lottery, giving them the top pick in the 1997 draft. They selected Duncan, the All-American from Wake Forest.

Because Robinson returned healthy in 1997-98, Duncan was not expected to save the franchise. He could develop at this own pace,

Duncan and Robinson formed a dynamic duo down low. Here they work their defensive magic.

Twin Talents

Robinson and Duncan complemented each other well. Each made the other's job easier. Plus, both could pop outside and shoot the jumper.

thanks to the presence of his future Hall of Fame teammate.

Robinson was not threatened by Duncan's arrival. He invited the recent draft pick out to his home in Aspen, Colorado, where they hung out together. Not only did they become great friends, but Robinson knew there would be someone very special across the lane from him.

Duncan won Rookie of the Month nearly every single month. He ran away with NBA Rookie of the Year honors with 21.1 points per game, 54.9 percent shooting, and 11.9 rebounds per game. He was named to the First Team All-NBA team, the first rookie to do so since Larry Bird.

"It makes my job so much easier when he can score like that on the block late in the game," said Robinson. "The

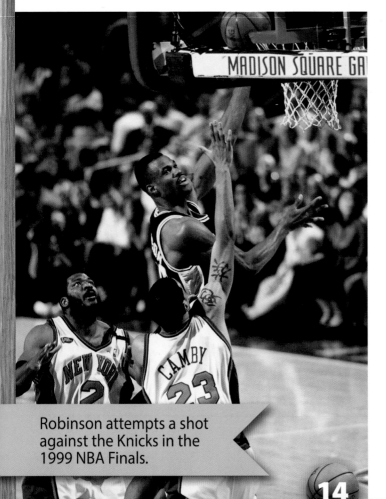

Robinson attempts a shot against the Knicks in the 1999 NBA Finals.

better he is, the more my game is going to flow."

Duncan figured it all out quickly, too. "We're smart enough players to figure out how much to complement each other without clashing too much."

The Twin Tower concept of two tall centers had been tried before in the NBA, but it never seemed to work. The reason: None of the duos had someone who could pop out and score away from the basket. The Spurs had two, in the 7'1" Robinson and 6'11" Duncan.

"Size does matter in this league, particularly in the playoffs," said Knicks coach Jeff Van Gundy. "And their size beat our speed and quickness."

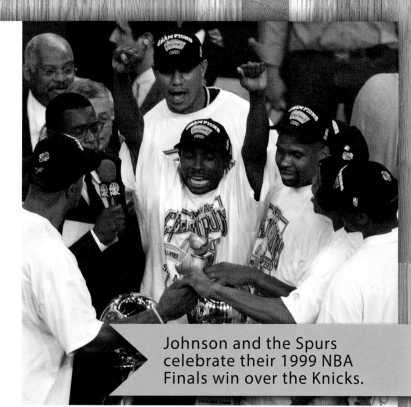

Johnson and the Spurs celebrate their 1999 NBA Finals win over the Knicks.

So even though it was "The Little General," Avery Johnson, who scored the Spurs' biggest basket in Game 5 of the 1999 Finals, size does matter in Texas. For the NBA team in San Antonio, bigger is better.

Size Beats Speed

According to New York coach Jeff Van Gundy, the Spurs' size beat the Knicks' speed and quickness.

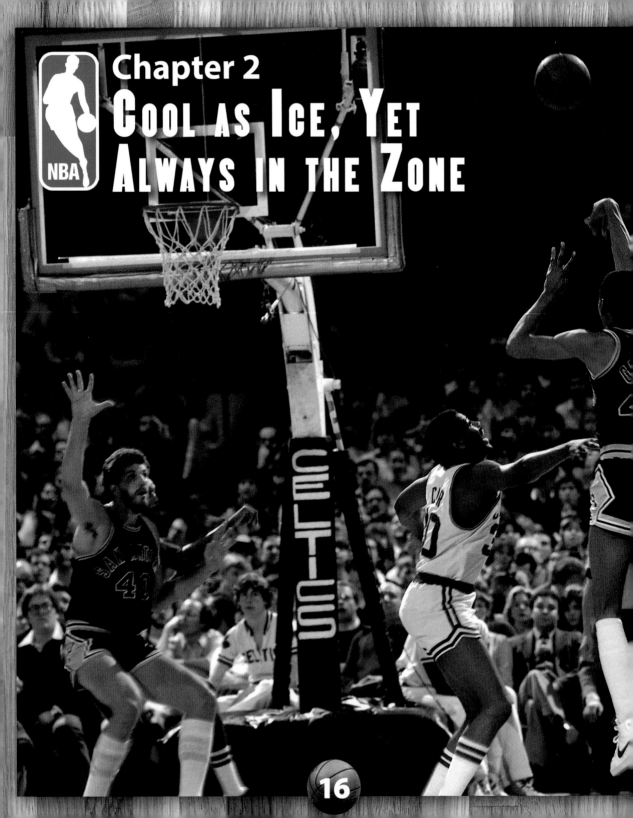

Chapter 2
Cool as Ice, Yet Always in the Zone

Avery Johnson was never a big scoring threat. But he was a leader, and he came up big when it mattered most.

From 1974 to 1985, the Spurs had another leader who came up big, time and time again—one who could shoot and score. His name was George Gervin, and he was called the "Iceman" because of his cool conduct on the court. He averaged over 20 points a game for 12 consecutive years.

His signature shot was the finger roll. He would cup the ball in one hand then flick it up and over a defender and into the basket. Capable of dunking, Gervin rarely did. His game was less about power and more about finesse. His style of basketball had a bit of artistry to it. He was smooth. The future Hall of Famer, who became the most recognizable Number 44 outside of Hank Aaron, was the face of the franchise for more than a decade.

But he was not yet there when the Spurs were born. One of the original 11 American Basketball Association (ABA) teams, the Spurs were actually the Dallas Chaparrals when they started in 1967-68. They experienced some success their inaugural season, sweeping the Houston Mavericks in the first round of the ABA playoffs. But they lost in the second round to the New Orleans Buccaneers.

Late in the 1972-73 season, the

The Iceman Cometh
George Gervin averaged over 20 points a game for 12 consecutive years and became a legend playing for the Spurs.

team was struggling to attract fans. No one in Dallas seemed to care about the Chaps. They were far out of the playoff hunt when it was announced that a group from New Jersey was interested in purchasing the club. At that point, any local interest in the team vanished. Then, to add to the team's misery, the Jersey deal fell through.

Thankfully, a group of business-men from San Antonio rescued the franchise. They agreed to purchase the team and move them south to San Antonio. In their last game at the Dallas Convention Center, the Chaps beat the Carolina Cougars, the best team in the ABA that year, 112-110. Only 134 people showed up to see it!

Things immediately got better 250-plus miles down I-35. Now called the Spurs (their first new name, Gunslingers, was scrapped before the season officially started), the team won its first game in the HemisFair Arena in front of 1,799 fans.

Thus began a love affair between the people of San Antonio and the Spurs. The Spurs are San Antonio's only professional sports franchise among America's big four sports (basketball, baseball, football, and hockey). Right from the beginning, San Antonio embraced its basketball team; their basic black, silver and white uniforms; and the players commitment to the city.

Go Spurs Go!

The city of San Antonio fell in love with the Spurs, the only professional sports team in town, from the beginning. The fans' rallying cry of "Go Spurs Go!" can be seen on signs all over the city.

Today, several former Spurs make their home in town and are active in the community. Robinson founded the Carver Academy, a culturally diverse public school near downtown. Meanwhile, George Gervin's Youth Center serves at-risk youth and disadvantaged families. The connection between the players and their city is almost unmatched in the NBA. In part because of this involvement, Spurs fans are among the most loyal in the league. The team set several attendance records while playing at the Alamodome, and continues to sell out the smaller AT&T Center. Signs sporting the Spurs' rallying cry of "Go Spurs Go!" can be seen all over the city.

For his signature shot, the finger roll, Gervin would cup the ball in one hand and flick it up and over the rim.

Back in 1973, within a month after arriving in San Antonio, the team had settled in—and things were looking up. Soon thereafter, they bought the rights to a 21-year-old Gervin from Virginia. Gervin joined the team in February to help

Gervin turned the Spurs into one of the highest scoring teams in NBA history.

up his rookie campaign with a taste of what Spurs' fans could expect, as he began to turn the club into one of the highest scoring teams in history. In the playoffs against Indiana, Gervin moved from forward to shooting guard and quickly raised the level of his game. In the final three games of the series, he averaged 35 points. But it wasn't enough; the Spurs lost once again, this time in six games.

When the 1975-76 season started, the ABA was down to seven teams playing in one division. While things looked dim for the league, San Antonio loved its new team. The Spurs boasted four players in the ABA All-Star Game. And they finished the year in third place with a 50-34 record.

the Spurs win 12 of its final 16 games and clinch third place in the Western Division. Unfortunately, they lost to the Indiana Pacers in seven games in the first round of the playoffs.

In 1974-75, the Spurs finished in second place in the Western Division with a 51-33 record. Gervin followed

Their first round playoff opponent turned out to be the New York Nets and "Dr. J," Julius Erving. The Spurs gave the good doctor all he could handle before losing 121-114 in Game 7. The Nets went on to claim the ABA's ninth and final championship.

The Spurs' good season and impressive performance against the Nets meant everything. On June 17, 1976, they were invited—along with the Denver Nuggets, Indiana Pacers, and New York Nets—to join the NBA, as the ABA folded.

But there were no championship banners raised by the Spurs over the next 20-plus years. Even though Gervin was setting records he ultimately became the first guard to win back-to-back NBA scoring

The Spurs' performance against Erving and the Nets earned them an invitation to join the NBA once the ABA folded.

titles), and the Spurs experienced success, they could never get past the Western Conference Finals. That was where the Spurs usually lost to the Los Angeles Lakers.

But another big man—or two—changed everything.

Disappointing Decades
Despite the fact that Gervin was setting records, the Spurs couldn't get past the Western Conference Finals for 20-plus years.

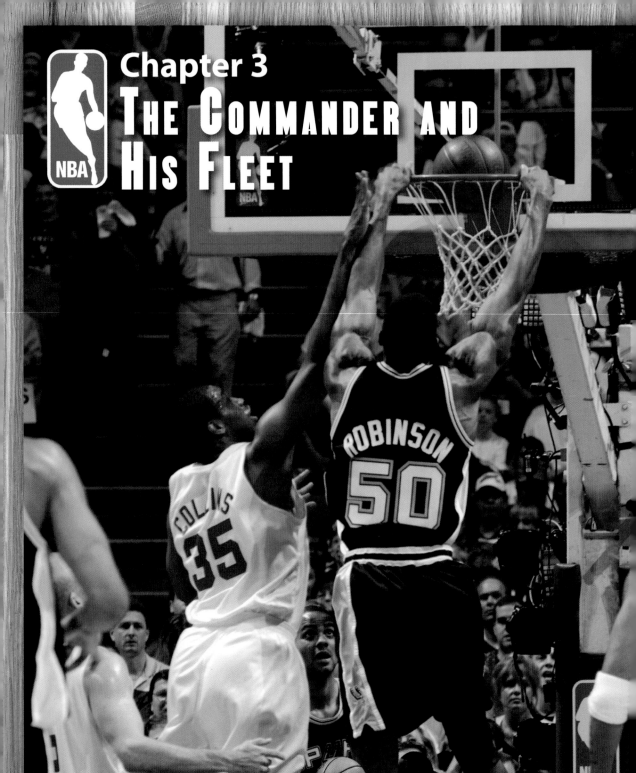

ROBINSON
50

COLLINS
35

The Spurs were awarded the top pick in the 1987 NBA Draft and chose David Robinson of Navy. Just 6′2″ when he entered the Naval Academy, Robinson was 6′11″ when he graduated. And by the time he joined the Spurs two years later, after serving his two-year military service commitment, he was 7′1″.

Hoping to captain a submarine some day, Robinson realized the Navy had no subs that could accommodate his size. So the NBA turned out to be a nice fallback for him. He joined the Spurs for the 1989-90 season and helped spark one of the greatest single-season turnarounds in NBA history.

After going 21-61 the year before, Robinson, along with rookie Sean Elliott and free agent acquisition Terry Cummings, led the Spurs to a 56-26 record and first-place finish in the Midwest Division.

The Admiral had one of the most successful rookie seasons

With their top pick in the 1987 NBA Draft, the Spurs selected David Robinson, an offensive threat and fearsome shot-blocker.

23

Elliott splits the Knicks' defense and lofts a short jumper. He was traded away in 1993 but returned just a year later.

Western Conference All-Star team, and was the unanimous choice for NBA Rookie of the Year.

Perhaps more importantly, the Spurs became a familiar face in the playoffs. In Robinson's rookie year, they took the Trail Blazers to Game 7 in a series that saw the Spurs lose two heartbreakers in overtime. They continued to make the postseason in subsequent years but were never able to make it to the Finals.

In 1993, the Spurs traded Elliott to the Pistons for Dennis Rodman, the NBA's premier rebounder. Rodman took the Spurs from worst in the league in offensive rebounding percentage to first

for a center in NBA history. In his debut, he scored 23 points and pulled down 17 rebounds. He was named NBA Rookie of the Month in every month of the season. Overall, he averaged 24.3 points and 12 rebounds a game, was named to the

His impact on Robinson was even greater. No longer feeling the pressure to rebound, the Admiral could venture out to the perimeter. As a result, he led the NBA in scoring with 29.8 points per game, taking the title away from the Lakers' Shaquille O'Neal by scoring 71 against the Clippers. In doing so, he became only the fourth player in the history of the league to score 70 points in a game. He and Rodman, who averaged 17.3 rebounds per game, became the first teammates to lead the NBA in both scoring and rebounding in the same season.

Inside Outside

With Rodman grabbing offensive rebounds, Robinson was able to venture out to the perimeter and shoot from outside. As a result, he led the NBA in scoring in 1993.

In 1994, the Spurs turned in a league's best 62-20 regular season record. Despite career seasons from Elliott (who returned to San Antonio)

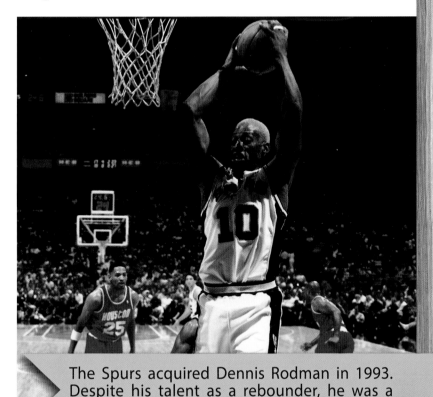

The Spurs acquired Dennis Rodman in 1993. Despite his talent as a rebounder, he was a distraction to the team and was ultimately traded.

Duncan slams one through the hoop in a game against the Jazz. With Duncan, the Spurs became the most improved team in NBA history.

the 1997-98 season with 56 wins to become the most improved team in NBA history—besting their previous record. In 1999-2000, they ended up losing again in the playoffs but made their share of headlines. Elliott became the first player to return to action after an organ transplant. (He received a new kidney the summer before.) Avery Johnson became the Spurs' all-time assists leader. Robinson played in his 710th game as a Spur, becoming San Antonio's all-time leader in games played.

With the championship in 1998-99, the Spurs had basically perfected their inside-outside game

and Robinson (who won the league MVP award), the Spurs weren't able to get over the hump in the playoffs. For all his talent, Rodman was a distraction, and it seemed the Admiral had taken the team as far as he could.

But with Duncan, everything was different. The Spurs finished and stingy defense. In 2000-01, they led the NBA in home attendance for the first time. And they made the playoffs again, for the 11th time in 12 seasons, but lost to the Lakers in the Western Conference Finals.

In 2001-02, the Spurs finished with the same record as the year before, 58-24. Duncan won the league MVP award and Robinson passed Gervin as the Spurs' all-time leading scorer. He scored his 20,000th point against Golden State, becoming the 27th player and 10th center in NBA history to achieve that milestone.

Also, 19-year-old Belgian-born, French-raised guard Tony Parker

Post-Season Poster Boys
In 2001, the Spurs made the playoffs for the 11th time in 12 seasons. Also that year, they led the NBA in home attendance.

became the youngest player to appear in a game in Spurs' history. Parker moved into the starting lineup. If not for the Lakers, the Spurs would have returned to the NBA Finals.

Belgian-born, French-raised Tony Parker became, at 19, the youngest player in Spurs' history.

Bruce Bowen prepares to fire a jumper against the Mavericks.

With Duncan winning the MVP again, Argentinian rookie guard Manu Ginobili making an immediate impact, the stars were aligned.

Winning more games than anyone in the league, the Spurs cruised through the playoffs. They beat the Suns, the Lakers, and then the Mavericks to get to the Finals, where they faced off against Jason Kidd and the New Jersey Nets.

At age 37, Robinson put an exclamation point on his 14-year career in storybook fashion. With a 3-2 series lead, the Spurs looked to close it out at home in Game 6. After starting slowly, Robinson ignited the Spurs during

They did the following year, a memorable one for the club. Before the season started, Robinson announced it would be his last.

a crucial 17-7 run in the second quarter. In a signature moment, Robinson blocked a shot by Nets forward Kenyon Martin, starting a fast break that resulted in a Bruce Bowen jumper that cut New Jersey's lead to 33-30. The Admiral added a driving layup moments later, snagged a key defensive rebound, and then took a charge from a driving Martin.

Robinson's heroics seemed to fire up the home arena crowd and his teammates. But he wasn't done yet. At the other end, he slipped inside for a high-post lob from Duncan and laid the ball in to cut the Nets' lead to 38-36.

With the championship in sight, and wanting to give their leader a going-away present, the Spurs really turned it on at the end. San Antonio went on a 19-0 run in the fourth quarter. The crowd went nuts as Robinson pulled down seven rebounds during this stretch and hit the only shot he took.

The Admiral, who was named by the NBA as one of its 50 Greatest Players, retired a champion with 13 points and 17 rebounds in his final game.

"My last game, streamers flying, world champions," said Robinson. "How could you write a better script than this?"

You couldn't.

A Storybook Ending

In 1996, Robinson was deemed one of the 50 Greatest Players in NBA History. He put an exclamation point on his 14-year career by winning his second NBA title with the Spurs.

obinson had retired, but the Spurs still had Duncan. At this point, he was not only one of the NBA's best offensive threats but perhaps its greatest defensive force. They also had Popovich, a coach who emphasized defense. And they had Parker, Ginobili, and Bowen, who played with energy on both ends of the court.

"For us," said Duncan. "Defense is first, second, third, and last."

And Duncan was the key to it all. He joined Robinson as the second player to be named to both an All-NBA team and an All-Defensive team in each of his first seven seasons in the

The Deacon of Defense
Under Popovich's scheme, Duncan, the former All-American for the Wake Forest Demon Deacons, excelled as one of the best defenders in the NBA.

league. To think he was headed for greatness as one of the world's best swimmers makes his feats on the basketball court all the more incredible. Born and raised on St. Croix, part of the U.S. Virgin Islands,

According to Duncan, shown here blocking a shot, defense was the key to the Spurs' success.

31

Duncan was training as a swimmer for the Olympics.

Things changed, though, when his mom was diagnosed with breast cancer. Then, in 1989, Hurricane Hugo damaged the pool where he trained. Unwilling to train in the ocean due to a fear of sharks and upset about his mom, who was his biggest fan, Duncan started skipping swim practice. Soon, he began drifting away from the sport. In April 1990, his mom died, and he never swam competitively again.

Fearing he would lose all interest in sports, Duncan's uncle convinced

Duncan grew up on the Caribbean island of St. Croix, in the U.S. Virgin Islands, where he posed for this photograph in 2005.

him to shoot some hoops. Because he thought Duncan would top out at 6'6", he taught him how to handle the ball, pass and shoot from the outside.

In 2004-05, he used those skills to bring the Spurs back to the NBA Finals, where they faced the defending champs, the Detroit Pistons. Detroit was coached by Popovich's mentor, Larry Brown.

After battling through blowouts, comebacks, and enough drama to last a lifetime, these two evenly-matched teams took the series to a Game 7. With what seemed like the whole world watching, including David Robinson at courtside,

the game was a classic. Every single possession became critical. Sticking to their defensive game plan, the Spurs were doing everything right, but they just couldn't pull away.

San Antonio missed its first six shots of the second half. The Pistons promptly went up by nine, thanks to Ben Wallace, Chauncey Billups, and Rip Hamilton. The arena was quiet,

Duncan was a world-class swimmer before he became a high-flying NBA superstar.

Duncan looks to pass the ball to Robert Horry in the Finals against the Pistons. According to Popovich, Duncan had decided the Spurs "were just not going to lose."

the Spurs fans tense with concern. Their team was falling apart before their eyes. The Spurs needed a spark.

Sensing the game was slipping away, Duncan rose to the challenge. He was determined to lead his team to victory. And just when the Spurs needed him most, he brought his A-game. He single-handedly took over the game, putting it all on his shoulders, demanding the ball and making the plays.

"Timmy decided we were just not going to lose," said Popovich.

Duncan was named Finals MVP becoming only the fourth player to win the MVP award three times.

"This trophy is definitely an honor but this team had so many MVPs," said Duncan. "There are so many different guys here who just laid it on the line. We couldn't have made it this far without any of them. So every one of them is an MVP."

Ginobili was one such candidate. Only the third player in the world to win an Olympic gold medal and an NBA ring in the same season, Manu brought a passion to the court that became contagious.

"I don't play like this because I want to look pretty," said Ginobili. "I think people can really see I love the game."

Ginobili helped draw attention to the fact that the Spurs featured six players born outside the United

No "I" in "Team"

There could have been any number of Spurs who took home the Finals' MVP, but the award went to Duncan, who became just the fourth player to be named MVP three times.

States on their championship roster. San Antonio became the face of the new NBA, which began experiencing what Ginobili called an

Ginobili, here making a reverse basket, brought a contagious passion to the court.

A Global Perspective

As the NBA experienced an "international boom," the Spurs led the way with a French and Argentinian backcourt, not to mention a Caribbean center

"international boom." With a French and Argentinean backcourt, a center from the Caribbean, the Spurs play the global game of basketball with an international flair. Their locker room is home to a host of different cultures, yet they make it work together, night in and night out.

International flair: Ginobili, from Argentina, looks to pass to Parker, a Belgian raised in France, in a game against the Nuggets.

Even more significant is how the Spurs always seem to find value in players that others don't. The list of such undervalued players includes Avery Johnson, George Hill, Parker 2011-12 rookie Kawhi Leonard, and Ginobili. The Spurs took Ginobili with the 57th pick and then let him mature in Spain for a few more years. Today, he is widely considered one of the top second-round picks in the history of the game. Since 1999-2000, San Antonio has had 13 consecutive 50-win seasons without having had a Top-20 pick in the NBA Draft. They have consistently found gems at the bottom of the first and into the second round. Second round selections in the NBA Draft usually amount to role players at best—and outright busts at worst.

Much of the credit for landing less expensive yet worthy talent goes to R.C. Buford, the Spurs'

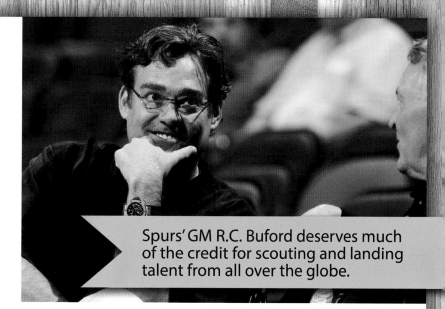

Spurs' GM R.C. Buford deserves much of the credit for scouting and landing talent from all over the globe.

senior vice president and general manager. It is Buford's vision and eye for talent that has helped build San Antonio into one of the most successful franchises in pro sports. As one of the NBA's small market teams, Buford doesn't look for high-priced free agents to support his key players. He looks for young talent (often late in the draft) and former players who are willing to re-sign (often for less money).

"He is always looking at the big

picture and long term. We never get ourselves in too awkward a position in terms of contracts or dollars so that we have flexibility, which is so hard to do these days," says owner Peter Holt. "We have the main three [Duncan, Parker and Ginobili], but we've always managed to bring the

"Moneyball"

The Spurs have always sought value in players that other teams aren't interested in. They have consistently found less expensive talent in the bottom of the first and into the second round of the NBA Draft.

Ginobili launches a jump shot.

right players in around them.

"We know what we are looking for—hard-working, high-character, team-oriented, mentally tough, coachable and unselfish players," said Buford. "There are NBA players who aren't necessarily Spurs, and there are Spurs who may not fit someplace else."

Even though the team failed to defend its crown in 2005-06, losing to the Mavs in the playoffs, the Spurs were back in 2006-07 to right that wrong.

In February 2007, the Spurs found themselves just 1.5 games out of third place. With the trade deadline approaching, Popovich had to decide whether it was time to break up the team. He chose not to, and the Spurs got hot.

They were an NBA-best 25-6 down the stretch, boasting the league's best defense.

After putting the Nuggets away in five, the Suns in six, and the Jazz in five, they returned to the Finals to face LeBron James and the Cleveland Cavaliers.

The Spurs showed they were the tops in the NBA by sweeping the Cavs. Parker penetrated, passed,

and scored his way to the NBA Finals MVP award. Back in Texas, fans threw confetti and honked their horns until dawn. A few days later, the city of San Antonio was treated to its fourth championship parade along the Riverwalk.

Over 300,000 San Antonians line the Riverwalk in celebration of the Spurs.

Every year, *ESPN The Magazine* ranks 122 professional sports teams from the NBA, NFL, MLB and NHL. In 2011, once again, the publication showed its love for the San Antonio Spurs.

ESPN ranked the Spurs fifth overall in the standings, and first among all 30 NBA teams. It was the sixth time the magazine put the Spurs atop all NBA franchises. San Antonio, in fact, is the only franchise to have been named the top overall team twice among the four major sports since ESPN introduced its annual survey in 2003.

The Spurs ranked No. 1 overall in two specific categories: "fan relations" (openness and consideration toward fans) and "players" (in particular, their likeability off the court). The city

The *Spurs Win!* flag got a workout in San Antonio as victories became commonplace.

Juggling Act

Faced with a rash of injuries in 2011-12, Popovich pieced together a 12-man roster of age and youth, chemistry and attitude.

of San Antonio absolutely loves its basketball team.

And why shouldn't they? In their 35 NBA seasons since 1976–1977, the Spurs have captured 18 division titles. They have made the playoffs in 21 of the last 22 seasons. They have won four NBA championships, more than any franchise except the Celtics, Lakers, and Bulls. And since 1980, only two other coaches have won more NBA titles than Popovich.

In 2011-12, as usual, the Spurs were back in the hunt. But the team suffered a rash of injuries, including Ginobili's fractured hand that

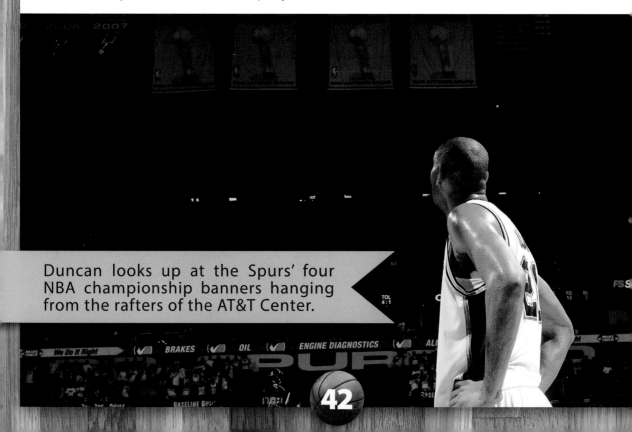

Duncan looks up at the Spurs' four NBA championship banners hanging from the rafters of the AT&T Center.

caused him to miss 22 games. Popovich faced perhaps the greatest challenge of his career. Piecing together a 12-man-deep roster of rookies and former NBA no-names, "Pop" juggled an extraordinary mix of age and youth, chemistry and attitude. He put Leonard into the starting lineup by midseason. Popovich relied on Brazilian Tiago Splitter to become his new pick-and-roll option. He called on Matt Bonner and Danny Green, two young players that other teams had given up on, to step up. Before the trade deadline, he brought back Stephen

Popovich inserted Kawhi Leonard, here scoring against the Clippers, into the starting lineup midway through the 2011-12 season.

Jackson, a key player on the 2003 championship team. And resting his "Big Three" of Duncan, Parker, and

Sheer Genius

In a bold move, Popovich rested his "Big Three" of Duncan, Parker, and Ginobili during the regular season. The goal was to keep the trio fresh for a deep run in the playoffs.

Popovich was awarded NBA Coach of the Year in 2012.

Ginobili was bold but effective.

For his mastery, Popovich won Coach of the Year. And Parker passed Johnson as the Spurs' all-time assists leader. By the end of the regular season, the Spurs

Winning Streak

Entering the playoffs as the No. 1 seed in the West, the Spurs won an NBA-record 20 straight games that extended from the end of the regular season through the first two games of the Western Conference Finals.

were everyone's pick to represent the Western Conference in the Finals. They entered the playoffs as the No. 1 seed for the second straight year. Their first-round exit last year at the hands of the eighth-seeded Memphis Grizzlies was a distant memory—especially after they swept the Utah Jazz and Los Angeles Clippers to extend their winning streak to an incredible 18 games.

In the conference finals, the Spurs extended the streak to an NBA-record 20 games with a pair of lopsided wins over the Oklahoma City Thunder. The Thunder looked immature in the first two games, as the Spurs took them to school time and again.

Then, everything changed. The Thunder began to play like seasoned veterans. Their "Big Three"—Kevin Durant, Russell Westbrook, and James Harden—outdid the Spurs "Big Three," who looked unsure of themselves… and suddenly old. The Thunder won Game 3 by 40 points, 102-82, forcing 21 San Antonio turnovers.

It happened again in Game 4, as OKC evened the series. The Spurs lost Game 5 as well, the first time they had dropped three games in a row all year. Then, the Thunder ended the Spurs' quest for a fifth NBA

Parker passed Avery Johnson as the Spurs' all-time leader in assists in the 2011-12 season.

championship. OKC rallied from 18 down to win Game 6, and the Western Conference title.

Duncan controls the ball against the Clippers.

Duncan. "That was our singular goal, but obviously it ends here."

"We had a wonderful season," Popovich said. "Everybody wants to be the last team standing, but in many ways this group may have ever overachieved."

The Spurs will no doubt need to tweak their roster, especially if they want to beat the "thunderous" storm brewing in the West.

"I thought this was our time to get back to the Finals and push for another championship," said

They just might have to do something big. Which is nothing new to the state of Texas… or to the Spurs.

Thunderous Collapse

After taking a two-games-to-none lead in the 2012 Western Conference Finals, the Spurs dropped four straight to the young and talented Oklahoma City Thunder.

Duncan drives past Channing Frye of the Suns.